Thanks for hm

Thanks
you for being
a light in a
dark place

HOW TO FIRE THE DEVIL
AS YOUR LIFE COACH!

How To
FIRE
The
DEVIL
As Your
LIFE COACH!

Why Christians **Fail** And How To **Stop**.

By
DESMOND ANTONIO BLACKBURN

Xulon Press

Xulon Press
2301 Lucien Way #415
Maitland, FL 32751
407.339.4217
www.xulonpress.com

Scripture quotations taken from the King James Version (KJV) – *public domain.*

Scripture quotations taken from the Holy Bible, New Living Translation (NLT). Copyright ©1996, 2004, 2007 by Tyndale House Foundation. Used by permission of Tyndale House Publishers, Inc.

Printed in the United States of America.

ISBN-13: 9781545621714

* I ___ Reyes will be the best husband to establish a better no matter what

* I ___ Reyes will be the best father to Edison Reyes → better no matter what

* I ___ Reyes will be a billionaire by age 45 or better no matter what

* I ___ Reyes will be a better father to Edison Reyes → better no matter what

* I ___ Reyes will love 60/60 and be an amazing ___ ___ better no matter what

Table of Contents

Dedication

To my parents Carlos and Celina Blackburn for their hard work and tireless devotion to encouraging their kids to do better. To my aunts, Meryl, Sheryl and Gloria Blackburn who kept my sister and I in church while managing to dress us up in uncomfortable shoes and ill-fitting clothing. To my sister for being my first supporter, cheerleader and advocate. To my "abuela," Lola Burnet who's "air cover" of prayer kept many of us from falling off the deep end. To my grandfather Milton Clark for always asking "Where's the book?" To every employer and pastor that I have met along the way. To RJM, who's campus outreach at California State University Northridge in the 90's came at a time when I needed protection from myself. To Apostle Beverly (Bam) Crawford, who gave me my first shot as a young author. To Dr. Earl Johnson, who's wisdom was invaluable during our season of transition. To Bishop Ed Smith and the entire Zoe congregation who have provided my family and I with a great place to worship and "try again" during our season of renewal.

I would also like to dedicate this book to my children, Kyle and Chloe Blackburn, who are a daily reminder of God's sense of humor. And most of all to my gift from God, Denine. I indeed have found a wife and have received favor from the Lord.

Lastly, I want to thank my God for every failure, mis-step and opportunity to grow along the way. Without your grace, mentorship and patience I don't know where I'd be, perhaps drinking milk at an Applebees wondering how everything went so terribly wrong.

THE DEVIL, THE ORIGINAL LIFE COACH
Introduction

"*ow to Fire the Devil As Your Life Coach"*, isn't just a clever title that was cooked up while in the shower, but a guide on how to fire the worst provider of advice since the beginning of time.

Like any decent life coach, the Devil listens to what you say, repeats what you just said and then positions what you've said in a form of a question. "Did God really say that you couldn't eat of all the trees in the garden?" Unfortunately, we know how this story goes, Eve eats the fruit, gives it to Adam and they are kicked out of the garden and forced to live a life of toil and hardship.

Now before we go on and solely blame the Devil for this situation, let's ask a question. How can two people who have everything be convinced to give it all up?

Adam and Eve could have felt on some level that God was holding out on them. My guess is that the enemy picked up on this sliver of distrust and went on a campaign to capitalize on this fear of being "held out on" and suggested that God isn't good and the only way to get what they wanted was to fire God and hire the Devil as their life coach. James 1:14-15 says "Temptation comes from our own desires, which entices us and drag us away, these desires give birth to sinful actions and when sin is allowed to grow, it gives birth to death"

The key here is that while the enemy is crafty and subtle it's our evil desires that seal the deal. So, here's the process: man has a subtle, yet dark idea. The enemy brings it to the forefront, gases up their desire to act on that idea and before you know it, they are knee deep in guilt, condemnation and shame. In the end you have no one to blame but yourself.

STOP!

We've been created to be better than this and if we have any hope of getting out of this "rinse and repeat" cycle of failure, then it's time we "Fire The Devil As Our Life Coach" and hire God and his word instead.

This book will take a creative and sometimes humorous look at why we fail as Christians and how we can stop. We will also learn how to stop becoming the enemy's unwitting pawns that do both the crime and the time. You will learn that Christians don't necessarily fail because of a spiritual attack from the devil, but from the acceptance of bad information coupled with a poor understanding of God's promises that manifest themselves into self-defeating habits.

To be clear, the Devil is real and while he is as crooked as they come, his job is to merely suggest ways for you and I to steal, kill and destroy ourselves and others. As sinister as that may sound, the fact is, none of his schemes can be accomplished without our full cooperation.

So, if you've decided that enough is enough and are willing to do what it takes to get out of your own way, then keep reading and get ready to shed the title of "victim" forever.

✱ I will will be a billionaire by age 40 or better no matter what.

Elder Kryp
101

Saved and Failing

I 've been in church all my life. As a child it seemed like I
lived at the altar. I was in all the Easter and Christmas
plays I attended vacation bible school, church picnics etc.
My friends were Christians, my family were Christians. Yep
"We love Jesus, yes, we do, we love Jesus how about you?"

I even remember walking up the church aisle to get
saved when I was only nine-years old. Of course, I had
no idea what I was doing but it seemed like an easy way
to earn some brownie points with my aunts and help my
pastor out by coming up to get "saved."

Growing up I never felt like the "cool kid" when going
to church. Out of all the feelings that I had about Jesus,
"winner," was not a word that I would use, hence my inse-
curity about telling my friends that I was a Christian. It
seemed like any mention of loss was associated with
Jesus. Hey, Aunt Betsy died. "I'll pray for you". We're out
of money, "let's go church". I lost my job, "Jesus will fix it."

1

Over time, I began to see Jesus as nothing more than a "break glass in case of emergency" kind of God. From where I was sitting it seemed like we had 10-times the spirituality and 5-times the lack. Even as a kid I could see that this math didn't add up.

Look I get it, helping the hurting and the needy is one of the reasons why Jesus came, but let's face it, the church has done a horrible job marketing the power of Jesus and every day church folk weren't helping. Every Sunday I saw the same type of people coming to worship. I saw the poor, the elderly, the recently paroled or someone who was experiencing some form of desperation. I also saw the socially awkward, the uninspired and unmotivated. If God's power was real, he apparently forgot to tell a few people.

When I became an adult, I'd hoped things would change. I went to college and after a period of being a black nationalist (another story), I rededicated my life back to God. Soon I was heavily involved in ministry, living with Christians, eating with Christians hanging out with Christians, you get the idea. Unfortunately, I saw it as a familiar pattern where everyone around me was either poor or struggling. Now granted, we were broke college students but if my prior experience was any indication of future events, my life was going to suck…in Jesus name.

Please do not get me wrong, money is not my sole measurement for judging one's ability to succeed or fail as a Christian. However, as I began to look around my community and that of others, I began to see that something was clearly out of whack. And then it dawned on me, I wasn't mad at the fact that Christians weren't doing better economically, I was mad because the (Christians) in my world, didn't seem to be making any real progress. We were stuck and not moving forward.

At church we were singing the same old songs and the names from the "sick and shut-in" list never came off. As the years went by, the only constant was that the young people left and the old and stuck were still, well, old and stuck.

As a Christian, things are supposed to be great. At least that's what we heard from the pulpit. We're supposed to be powerful and "No devil in hell can stop us!" But my reality was anything but that. At age 28 I was broke and in debt. I had no love-life to speak of, my career was in shambles and nothing that I was doing was working. To top it off I was living in a house with six other Christian men and I never felt more alone.

I was the definition of broke, busted and disgusted. Then in 1999, everything changed. While house sitting for a friend I used my weekend alone to have it out with God. I wanted answers and I wasn't going to leave until I got them. What would happen after that was nothing short of transformational.

God revealed all the things that I was doing to block Him from giving me his best. As a Christian, I was literally sabotaging his success with my bad habits, lack of basic discipline, carelessness, unteachableness and pride. I was also walking in an area of unforgiveness which led to an unhealthy level of sensitivity that had me offended at everything and everyone. I was a complete mess, all while attending worship, leading bible study and teaching in children's church. Thankfully I was set free after my encounter with God that weekend and my life has never been the same since.

This book is written for every believer who wants to get out of their own way and step into their greatness. So be encouraged, you're not cursed or destined to failure, you're just blocking your own path by taking some bad advice from the worst life coach in human history, the Devil. It is my belief that by the end of this book that you will become closer to operating within God's grace and looking more and more like the best version of yourself.

No Love No Victory

===

I put this up front for a reason. If you can't get pass an area of unforgiveness, then there's really no point on going any further. If my only goal were to sell a lot of books, I'm sure that my publisher would advise that I bury this subject somewhere in the middle. Thankfully that is not my only goal. I want to help Christians get out of their own way and when it comes to the weapon of choice for today's "self-saboteur" nothing does the job better than good old fashion unforgiveness and grudge holding.

I don't have a ranking for top ten poisons for today's Christian, but if I did, I would put unforgiveness at the very top. I remember in the 90's when I was going through a five-year period of pure failure. Everywhere I turned included some form of uncertainty or doubt. My first effort to be an entrepreneur took a dive, I quit college to run my business full time and four-years later I had no business, no degree and not a lot of options.

During this time, I remained active in my church. But along the way I allowed myself to get offended by one of the leaders in the ministry that I was attending. For several hours each day I would meditate on why I was right and how they were wrong. I would think about the offense so often that I was even dreaming about it while I slept. What I didn't know was that my small offense had now become a blistering wound of unforgiveness, which made it impossible to walk in love.

For the next five-years my life was a ball of confusion, quarrels and general unpleasantness. This was not God's will for my life, and for many Christians our string of failures both professional and personal begin and end here.

My unforgiveness totally inhibited my ability to truly love according to I Corinthians 13:4-8 (Living). *"Love suffers long and is kind, it is patient, not irritable, proud, rude and keeps no record of being wronged."* Because of my failure to walk in love, I became an emotional piñata and the enemy was getting in his batting practice both early and often. Unforgiveness affected my health, my money and my mind.

It's so clear to me now. How can any Christian expect to have victory without walking in Love? Love is a

7

condition that cannot exist or manifest while in a state of unforgiveness.

I'll never forget the freedom of ending my personal feud with that church leader. It felt like I lost 100lbs of emotional baggage in just 48-hours. And after five-years of slow-to-no progress, my life experienced a supernatural acceleration which led to a new job, a completed college degree and a marriage that has been successful for the past 16-years. Christians are failing and don't even realize that one of the prime suspects is unforgiveness.

So, what can I do about it?

First things first, identify the exact source of the offense. If you can't remember, ask a friend, family and or ask the Lord to show it to you. Sometimes it may take counseling to help you find it.

It's important that you find the "Ground Zero" of the offence and when it started. Like an outbreak, the source of a pandemic must be found if there is any chance of finding a cure. I recommend a great book on this subject written by Deborah Pegue, "*Forgive, Let Go and Live.*"

Next, attack unforgiveness with the word of God

I Cor 13:4-11 and Psalm 119:165 are just a few scriptures that I've personally used, but you don't need to collect a lot of passages to be effective. Quality not quantity wins the race here. It is better to have two to three scriptures that you have a revelation on than to have 25 verses memorized but have no power.

You may need several rounds of this in order to release your heart and your emotions from the offense. The key is to study his promises and confess them over your life both day and night. Forgiveness is not knowledge, it's a revelation that transcends from knowing something academically to having your own Ah-Ha! moment.

IMPORTANT POINT: This doesn't have to be a long process. (Although results do vary) I was healed in 48-hours, not because I'm God's favorite (which I am) but because I was 100% committed to doing anything and everything to get healed. I abandoned all my thoughts and opinions on who was right or wrong. I was an empty bucket and I only wanted Him to fill me up.

Not dealing with the source of the offense is like putting a band-aid on a gushing wound. No amount of "I'm sorry sessions" will solve this problem. Once the root cause of the offence is released by you, then love can come on in and have its perfect work. Notice what I said, "released by you." not them, you.

For Christians, this is huge. Ministries and families within churches have inadvertently influenced others with the lie that if we've "hugged it out" or had a big confession session that all is well. Now I'll admit, watching two people hug it out makes for good drama but drama doesn't heal people, forgiveness does.

"True forgiveness is a door that can only be opened from the inside out." – Nelson Mandela

This process of reconciliation is an "Inside-out" process, not an "outside in" procedure. Do the work on the inside first and the recovery and restoration will begin to manifest itself very quickly.

How would I know that I'm healed?

When the mere mention of the person's name no longer fills you with anxiety and is replaced with either love, empathy or no emotional response at all. The offense can truly be something that simply happened at one point in your life. When this occurs, you'll know that you are moving in the right direction and the Agape kind of love (love by decision) is operating in you.

WARNING! Do not glance over this. IF YOU DO NOT WALK IN FORGIVENESS every piece of advice to follow will be pointless. If you are walking in anger and unforgiveness on any level as a Christian please know that failure is all but guaranteed.

To be clear, unforgiveness will affect your money and every metric in which you judge success. To help you move towards unforgiveness, please follow the steps below.

1. Declare this over yourself (Out Loud) "It's my responsibility to walk in forgiveness."

2. List all the people who have hurt or offended you, alive or dead and see yourself forgiving them. Then, when ready, reach out to those that you've offended and take total ownership for your part in the conflict. In most cases the other party is clueless that they've offended you. The key is to take ownership and apologize for the part that you've played in the conflict. This can be tough, so feel free to work with a pastor, friend or coach to help support you during this time.

3. List all the people that you've hurt or offended, alive or dead and start by forgiving yourself. Then for those who are still alive, apologize. If you can't do it in person or by phone, write a sincere letter or send an email. Again, take total ownership without

the justification. This exercise has been incredibly effective in not only releasing you but in releasing others into a place of healing and restoration.

4. Now list all of the things that are not happening or going well in your life. Seeing my growing list of incomplete projects and failures on paper was an eye-opener. I didn't want to be a loser and seeing this list was the kick in the butt that I needed to do something about my unforgiveness.

5. Now begin to imagine what you would be doing if you weren't operating in unforgiveness.

6. Now begin to read and meditate on God's word in this area. This is huge. You can't get fuel from an empty tank.

Every circumstance is different but the more yielded you are to do what it takes to get healed, the faster your recovery. The determining factor is when God's promises goes from just "head knowledge" to a personal revelation.

Forgiveness doesn't happen when you get together with the offended party, forgiveness happens in your heart well before your encounter. Whether they choose to admit their part in the offense or accept your apology does not matter, you're free. If they want to keep the grudge going, it is now their problem and no longer yours. Feel free to pray for them, albeit from a distance.

BAD CODE

66 **M**oney doesn't grow on trees. Take care of the pennies and the dollars will take care of themselves. They may be rich they ain't happy. It's easier for a camel to go through the eye of a needle than a rich man to enter into heaven."

If you've grown up around family, been part of a team or went to church, chances are at some point you may have heard some of the phrases that were mentioned above regarding money.

If you think about it, you've heard a lot of things over the years regarding how to handle friends, business, ethnic groups etc. Some of these sayings have been permanently etched into your mind. What's funny is that you didn't necessarily believe what was said at first, but because you heard it so often, it went from a passing thought to becoming part of the collection of beliefs that have become hard-wired into your mind. As a result, that hard-wiring has become instrumental in how you see yourself and the world around you.

Some people, when asked, don't even know why they think the way they do. It's what mama thought, coach thought, what my pastor thought and now, it's what I think. These quaint sayings, ole wives' tales and family mottos have become the filters to how we see and relate to the world. And good or bad, they've shaped what we say and do.

Not all of these quaint sayings and beliefs are bad. In fact, many of them have helped steer entire generations toward the greater good. *"The early bird gets the worm" "Do unto to others what you would have them do to you." "cheaters never prosper."* etc. These beliefs and group norms are more than just quaint sayings but a form of healthy code that's been hardwired into the programming of our hearts and minds.

However, while there is good code there is also bad code, hardwired pre-programmed norms and thoughts that are so entrenched into our thinking that new thoughts and facts are automatically rejected whenever any thing challenges the pre-programmed norm. Let's take two groups. One believes that all Muslims are terrorist and the other is a

15

Muslim family that lives down the street. The Muslim family are tax paying Americans who have children that are well liked and excel in school. The father is an accountant and the mother is a business owner in town. The whole family was born and raised in the United States. Their religion happens to be Islam.

Bob's belief that all Muslims are terrorists is a hard-coded piece of bad code that came as a direct result of 9/11. Since then, he's been a frequent listener of radical right-wing talk shows that spew anti-muslim rhetoric. But Bob knows this family personally. He sees for himself that none of the things said about muslims are true, but despite their reputation for being good people, Bob encourages others to ridicule and cyber-bully muslim-americans.

In this situation Bob's bad code of ethnic and religious prejudice is so dominant that although he's been given good code to contradict his bad intelligence, his bad code rejects it. We've made the mistake of thinking that new code, new habits and new thoughts can co-exist with bad code, bad habits and bad thoughts, they cannot.

When you receive a system update or install the latest 2017 software on your computer, what do you think is happening? The bugs, viruses or malware that existed in the

2016 version are overwritten and rendered obsolete by the new code in the latest software.

In the case of Bob, the only way for him to remove the "bad code" that was fueling his fear and prejudice would have been to immerse himself with correct data over time or as the bible says in (Ephesians 4:23) "And be renewed in the spirit of your mind." If Bob got to know that family better, talk to other Muslims and challenge his prejudice with facts, over time, Bobs "bad code" would eventually become overwritten.

Another example are people that are desperate for a financial breakthrough. They buy the books, attend the seminars and even get personal coaching from top financial professionals. They get great results for a season and then, suddenly, their back into their old habits. They tell themselves "You only live once, you can't take it with you. He who dies with the most toys wins." Before long they are overspending, and under-saving and the cycle of debt begins again.

A young woman from a poor community works hard in school and becomes the first in her family to get a college degree. Eventually she graduates and lands a great paying job. However, while other co-workers are saving and investing by using a company stock program, she refuses to learn how. Her reason, "I'm not a financial expert. stocks and investments are for rich people, not people like me." This person is willing to lose thousands of dollars because of the errant beliefs that were founded on nothing more than conversations heard around the dinner table by people who knew very little about money.

So How Can I Override This Bad Code?

Conventional thinking has taught us that it takes 21-days to break a habit and that's true, but did you know that it takes 63-days to create a new lifestyle or way of thinking? According to Dr. Carolyn Leaf, author of "How To Retrain Your Brain," she demonstrates that repetitive actions and ways of thinking create neuro-pathways in your brain. Like new code in a computer, the size and strength of this new pathway takes time and 63-days of intentional thinking causes the old pathways to be minimized and rendered useless while the new neuro-pathways in the brain get stronger.

This is why diets don't last, racist keep hating and why we can't stay out of debt. We must intentionally build the healthy habits that create these neuropathways over a 63-day period-of-time or the changes will fail to stick and fall victim to the size and strength of the old neuro-pathway created by the old habits.

This is great news! Who would have thought that you can take years of bad thinking and clean it up in just 63-days! Self-doubt, unbelief, smoking, obesity. The list goes on and on. People who've done this have seen a complete shift in how they act and think. A person who commits to 63-days of no sugar now finds that they have no cravings for it even when surrounded by their favorite treats. Their newly created habits of eating healthy snacks has them preferring fruit over candy.

So I'm cured, right?

Not exactly, according to Dr. Leaf, your enjoyment of sugar is still there, your ability to smoke, watch porn and sin are all still there. But the size and strength of your neuropathway of heathy habits and beliefs are simply larger and stronger than the other pathways that were associated with those bad habits.

Again, great news! but a word to the wise, you must stay on top of your new habits. You see, those old habits didn't go anywhere they were simply overwhelmed and shut out. Think of it this way. You come into a dark room and turn on the light. When this happens the darkness instantly disappears. Where did it go? The darkness hasn't gone anywhere. For the moment, the darkness is being overwhelmed by the light, but turn off the light and the darkness returns.

So, what are we saying? We need to DOMINATE the areas of our thinking and our faith with both the word of God and intentional actions needed to obtain mastery in any area. Many Christians would stop here and interpret this to mean that all they need to do is meditate on scripture. That would be a mistake.

If the area is getting out of debt, for example, begin by studying God's word about his thoughts on debt. In addition to that, enroll in an online money management course, find phone apps that help you control your spending, join a Facebook accountability group; you get the idea. We all know what it's like to feel overwhelmed, well it's time to turn the tables and overwhelm your problem area with a multi-pronged attack of intentional actions that comes from all angles.

I did the math and according to the 63-day rule you can transform up to six major areas in your life in one year. Imagine being able to completely change your life by solving six major problems a year! Now you can finally get over that divorce and forgive your spouse, break the family tradition of creating debt, get to your goal weight, finish that degree, write that book, start that business or stop smoking for good.

So let's recap.

1. Find out what the word says about the area you want to change then choose one or two scriptures to both meditate on and confess out loud.

2. Declare it physically. Use your body to openly declare what the "Word" says and how you will think going forward. Really get into it, move, raise your voice, embrace your inner drill sergeant. Get in the mirror and begin to declare the facts outlined in God's word to you. Remember your old thoughts have been taking center stage in your head for a while and will not go unless they've been bombarded and forcefully removed.

3. List 5-10 ways that this new thinking will give you pleasure.

4. List 5-10 ways that the old thinking will continue to bring you pain.

Be sure to "rinse and repeat" the new vision at least 10 to 15-minutes every day for 63-days. If you treat this as a one-time thing you will lose. Remember, your errant thoughts and imaginations didn't just come overnight they've had an opportunity to embed themselves into the recesses of your mind for years.

Your daily dose of getting in the word and over-powering your old thoughts with specific scriptures will make all the difference in helping create a single message that will allow your brain and your new confessions to have the desired affect for change. Also seek out subject matter experts who can provide practical teaching and instruction on the very area that you are trying to change. I'm a big fan of Dave Ramsey and his philosophy on debt but there are many experts who can speak to this area. YouTube is a great resource for quick instructional videos from a host of experts in just about any area of interest.

WARNING: Your old thoughts and patterns will not go quietly. You will literally feel your body and mind resist your new habits and actions. When you begin to read and study again, suddenly you'll begin to feel sleepy. After a work-out, you'll have the biggest craving for ice cream. These reactions are not coincidence or your imagination this is your body's attempt to maintain the status quo. Ignore these urges, they will eventually get in line but only if they are forced to do so.

Not Enough

"I've tried everything I just don't understand why it didn't work out for me." Sound familiar? Just about everyone on the planet has uttered the above phrase at some point in their lives. As a person who's had his personal challenges with weight loss I can relate to the above statement. You are "Gung Ho" and excited. You purchase your gear and resolve to eat right and exercise.

Like Richard Simmons on steroids, you awkwardly twist, jump and sweat to up-beat music for three days straight. You tell yourself that you've obviously lost weight and fully expect the scale to agree with your version of the facts. The moment of truth arrives, and you step on the scale. It turns out that you've lost nothing. You storm off in disbelief and declare that all diets are stupid as you cry over a pint of Cherry Garcia.

So why did this person fail? They were eating correctly and were exercising. What happened? They were doing the "right things" they just were doing it enough.

I strongly believe that we have the answers to solve just about every challenge that we are facing right now. If you were to survey the folks in your church you would find that just about everyone knows how to lose weight, make money, pray, fast and get new members. You'd also find that this same group would claim that not sticking with their goals long enough was the main reason why they failed to get any results.

In the book "Outliers", the author Malcolm Gladwell theorizes that it takes about 10,000 hours of intentional practice in order to obtain mastery in just about anything. While many continue to debate this theory, the one thing that is without debate is that we are not doing enough of what we already know to do.

If I could see in the spirit I am willing to bet that I would see a world filled with both mentally and spiritual obese men and women who are literally constipated with incredible talents, abilities and know how. Imagine a city full of people who are walking around consuming new ideas, buying new books and hopping from seminar to seminar with the sole intent to learn but no execute on what they know. This is what James 1:22 meant when he said to be "Doers of the word and not hearers only, **deceiving** your own selves."

I am literally repenting as I write this. While some would say that I've done some pretty cool stuff over the years, I know my secrets and you know yours. You and I are living way below our means and I don't just mean money. We are holding out and have refused to unleash the fullness of what we are capable of. Come with me for a moment and ask yourself…

- Are you doing enough of what you know to do?
- What if you kept going and didn't stop until you got the desired outcome?
- What if you did it afraid?
- What if you stopped asking for permission?
- What if you hung out with some serious achievers?
- What if you weren't afraid to die trying?
- What if you stopped making excuses?

Say these words out loud and allow this to be your confession:

"Lord I repent right now for living below the talents and God given capabilities that you've given me. I give myself permission to both dream and do. Fear is no longer my hall pass for less than enough living. I now see that I can die doing what I hate, so I will dedicate myself to live doing what I love. I will not. I will not, I will not stop doing enough until I have achieved my desired outcome. You've already given me the tools. It's time to go to work. In Jesus name, amen"

Exercise:

Tell two people about your rededication and invite them to hold you accountable. Secondly take one goal (for now) and commit to doing everything to accomplish that goal. Use one that can be accomplished in 30-days. Provide a scheduled end-date and share that with your accountability team. Meet with your team weekly and check in.

Lastly, if you can't be relied on to push yourself to do enough, ditch the "guilt trip" make the adjustment and get help. If it's weight loss, then get a trainer, if it's finishing a book, going to school or applying for a new career, then get a coach. Contact me via facebook or go to <u>www.lay-offproof.com</u> and I'll schedule a coaching session with you.

Whatever you do, do something. There are <u>no acceptable excuses</u> for not doing enough to get the results you deserve.

Stop Winging It And be intentional

"And the Lord answered me and said, write the vision and make it plain upon tablets, that they may run that readeth it." (Habakkuk 2:2)

To have a compelling purpose begins with a compelling vision. Those with clear intent have a compelling reason. "You don't get what you want, you get what you MUST have"- Tony Robbins

Those with a clear vision of their destiny have strong intentions. To them it is not a question of "will I succeed" but a matter of "when I succeed." Clear intentions are just symptoms of a strong "Must Have."

Oscar's childhood was full of memories in which he and his siblings would go hungry because his mom often had to choose between paying rent or shopping for groceries. Oscar's mom was an immigrant and her salary as a hotel maid was never enough. Everyday Oscar would see men and women who had graduated college coming in and out of the hotel that his mother worked in. Seeing education as his ticket to bring his family out of poverty, Oscar set his sights on graduating college.

He attended school, avoided trouble and worked to save for his college tuition. He studied hard, got great grades and attended a local university. He graduated with a degree in business. Oscar's first job offer came with a great salary, car and housing allowance. Now his mother cooks every day and his family no longer must choose between food and housing.

Oscar's "must" for getting out of poverty and providing for his mother and siblings allowed him to be intentional in his efforts to eliminate distractions and not stop until he got his desired result.

In the bible we see that Jesus's intentions were clear from the age of 12 . Despite his youth he was constantly learning in the temple, working and training. This wasn't random. Preparation is strategy and although this may seem obvious to most, it isn't. Preparation that is not founded in purpose simply becomes a meaningless "to do" list. Don't fall for the trap, victory loves preparation. Those who would try to make the case that all you need to do is trust God and don't bother with being intentional haven't read this thing called the bible.

- Proverbs 21:5: "Good Planning and hard work lead to prosperity, but hasty shortcuts lead to poverty."
- Proverbs 24:27: "Do your planning and prepare your field before building your house."
- Proverbs 16:3: "Commit your ACTIONS to the Lord and your plans will succeed."

The strategy of the enemy is to get you and I to willfully abandon our paths to becoming intentional in our effort to prepare. We've all heard the collective voices in our head that say, "It's too hard, who do I think I am, I've got nothing to prove, it doesn't take all that, what's the point, the system is rigged."

The con game is to get you and I out of focus and onto a merry-go-round of useless activities that mascaraed as important tasks. "But Desmond, what if those tasks are important?" Here's the qualifier. If those tasks are not connected to your mission or desired outcome, then it is a waste of time and has become a distraction.

Please note, you don't get points for being busy, you get points for getting the job done and that will never happen unless you are mission focused with strong intentions.

You're NEVER going to feel like it, ever!

If being intentional and focused is relatively new to you, then you would probably assume that you could expect help from your own mind and body, right? After all, why would you work against yourself? I'm not trying to be a "wet blanket" here, but you need to give up on the fantasy of waiting to "feel like it."

You're never going to feel like saving for retirement, feel like eating Kale and Spinach, feel like refusing that extra donut, feel like studying, feel like apologizing etc. Holding out for this emotion is a waste of time. There are millions of people around the world who have failed to follow through on their ideas because they're hoping and praying that someday they'll feel like it. In her book "The 5 Second Rule, Mel Robbins proclaims that "motivation is garbage."

Robbins makes the case that our brain is hard-wired to keep you from doing anything that it has not deemed as comfortable or safe. "Our brains are wired to help us survive, not thrive." Whenever you deviate from your regular habit pattern of work, kids, TV and then bed, your brain begins to re-direct you back to the acceptable habits that have already been approved as "safe."

Therefore, you begin to feel sleepy when you attempt to read a book instead of watching television or suddenly experience joint and back pain the moment you decide to exercise. This is your brain's attempt to keep you safe by sending signals to your body telling it to stop this new activity and revert to the acceptable pattern of behavior.

So what can I do?

You're going to have to "Force It," Your brain must be conditioned to recognize that this new activity is safe. A great way to ease your brain into accepting new changes is to break up tasks that can be completed in 10-minutes or less.

It is said that the founder of IKEA Ingvar Kamprad uses this rule for just about everything including company meetings. By using a smart phone or timer on his watch, he would budget a task to be completed in under 10 minutes. This tactic is not only effective in completing tasks quickly, but it's helpful in introducing your brain to new ideas and habits without it going into a protective mode. This 10-minute rule has been a life saver particularly for millennials. Let's face it, for many, having to focus for an entire hour without updating Instagram is a non-starter for some people.

So what's the take-a-way? Break down your ability to focus on becoming more intentional by doing so in 10-minute intervals. This will go a long way in helping you to force your brain to see things differently. Lastly, you need to settle on this fact, that anything that is beneficial and healthy will be met with resistance, not by the "haters" but by your mind and your emotions, so plan accordingly.

Another way to stop winging it and become more intentional is to become fully persuaded. Being all in, passionate and fully convinced is a powerful force that will help you maintain momentum while building your vision. Unfortunately, that level of conviction is rarely found in most people. This explains why so many of us tend to lose interest in the projects that we're working on in exchange for the "new shiny thing."

There's a reason for that.

People who do "random," are perceived by some to have an adventurous life. They are comfortable with going with the flow, meeting interesting people, picking up unique facts and hearing new stories. For people who lack variety and have been protected by the discipline of routine, this level of randomness can be appealing. But here's the punchline, while attractive at first, the constant uncertainty created by random and unintentional living, leads to a purposeless life that is full of uncertainty and riddled with fear.

This is why girls go for the "bad boy". The randomness of the lifestyle and the deviation from accepted norms are exciting and sexy at first. However, over time, if that lifestyle remains random and uncertain, It begins to lose its appeal and the "bad boy" persona is soon rejected and a partner that doesn't have to be bailed out of jail or who can keep a job, is preferred.

Intentional living can lead to a life of significance. When you know your "why" and its value you don't feel lost. This way of thinking can literally save your life and is a major weapon against the feeling of worthlessness and depression.

Example: A young swimmer dreams of someday competing in the Olympics and winning a gold medal. The intentional living of a structured diet, studying and training keeps that person focused, while other things like dating and extra activities are rejected and seen as a distraction.

Are you being intentional?

Give The Very Thing You Need

"Give and it shall be given, pressed down shaken together and running over shall men give to your bosom" (Luke 6:38)

For years we have heard this scripture touted from the pulpit (usually around offering time). We sing and often use it, but what people don't know is that this isn't just a scripture but a powerful strategy that is used to gain access to God's abundance

Now you may know that in your head, but if it doesn't become a revelation to you you'll walk around in as much stinginess as a person who doesn't know God

We've bought the lie that there are shortages and if we hoard and protect resources like our time, money and energy then we win. But that's a lie THERE ARE NO SHORTAGES! I get the same 24-hours as everyone else does, to build and create. There are no shortages of success, energy, love, joy or faith, the true building blocks of success. Now granted, man has created shortages to manipulate markets and drive up prices but that's a manifestation of man's evil and not God's perfect will for our lives.

Hopefully you can begin to understand why the idea of giving the very thing you need is so counterintuitive to how the world works. Normally when there is a physical, emotional or spiritual need the natural response of the flesh is to find a way to keep and hoard. "This is mine, get your own."

In God's economy, giving creates an environment that allows God to show up in the situation and creates a multiplication effect that surpasses anything that we could have gotten on our own. Case in point. (Mark 6:38) A little boy donates his lunch to the disciples who were trying to feed over 5,000 people. Jesus blesses it and not only are the people fed but there were several baskets of food that are left over for the boy to take home to his family.

(1 Kings 17:16) Elijah the prophet meets a woman who is down to her last batch of corn meal and oil for her and her son. She planned on cooking their last meal before they died. Out of obedience to the prophet she takes her last bit of food and feeds the prophet and themselves. Empowered by God, Elijah blesses her oil and meal jar

and as a result, she never runs out of meal or oil until the end of the famine. How's that for a return on investment?

These aren't just quaint stories but a clear under-standing of how things work when you decide to partici-pate within God's economy. As Christians, we are failing in our understanding of how He works and are toiling unnec-essarily hard. We are getting one-to-one ratios of returns when he intends for His people, who are called by his name, to walk in a lifestyle of multiplication in which we are getting 1000-to-1 rates of return.

(Ephesians 3:20) AMP "Now unto him who is able to carry out his purpose and do super abundantly more than we dare ask or think. Infinitely beyond our greatest prayers hopes and dreams according to his power that is at work within us."

By becoming free of this shortage mentality, we begin to find the very things that we need. We put an end to destructive self-consciousness and begin to witness the power of God to affect every area of our lives that matter.

Christians are blocking themselves from these prom-ises due to their willingness to accept the misinformation put out by the enemy. This mindset of lack, poverty and need has been interwoven into the fabric of religion and has led many to believe that low producing progress is sanctioned by God as part of his plan to achieve true holiness. I could not disagree more.

For centuries factions such as Franciscan monks and their vows of poverty have unintentionally promoted that true devotion to God can only happen if you are impoverished and live a life of solitude and financial poverty. Unfortunately, the world has deemed this as the only way that Christians should live and any efforts to do more are seen as un-Godly.

I fail to see how hooded males living in silence within a secluded monastery will help change the world for Christ in 2018. No disrespect to the order of Franciscan monks, but it's a little hard to believe that this is a lifestyle that that would minister to today's generation of believers. The world needs to see whole (complete) people who are walking in John 10:10: "I (Jesus) have come that they might have life and that they might have it more abundantly."

Mindsets and beliefs aside, giving the very thing you need is one of the most powerful offensive weapons that I have come to learn as a Christian. A few years ago, the technology company that I worked for brought on a new CEO. In the technology arena, prior experience has taught me that hires like this normally meant that my "days were numbered." Typically, new executives have shown a tendency to layoff the employees hired by the previous administration.

For weeks, I acted and thought poorly about the management. I even began to interview with other companies. My plan was to get out before they decided to let me go. You know, get them before they get me. (shortage mentality at work)

One morning, while in prayer, the Lord told me to pray for both my job and to specifically pray for the new CEO and his family. Hold on! What?

After a few moments of digesting what I believe I heard, I yielded, and began to pray that this new CEO would operate in wisdom and that he would prosper along with the health and well-being of his children. This went on for about a week. What would transpire afterwards was nothing short of amazing.

Not only was I not fired, but I was promoted, given prime territory and was publicly praised by the same management that I thought no longer valued me. I gave the very thing I needed. I prayed God's favor and blessing over my management and I personally received a boat-load of grace and favor in return.

So why did this work? was God simply replying to a well-orchestrated group of prayers. No. Giving what I needed got me out of a shortage mentality and back into God's promise to take care of me and the needs of my family. This tactic got me to re-direct my focus back to God and not the company.

In the end, this move activated the multiplication power of God's grace and allowed me to prosper in ways that I could not have predicted. I have since used this "Weapon of Warfare" several times and it has not ceased to fail me yet. I would strongly recommend this as your weapon of choice when dealing with confrontation. You'll get a few looks but trust me, it will be hard to argue with the results.

Exercise:

Identify a need in your life right now, marital, profes- sional, physical or financial. Now switch from "Why am I not receiving to "How can I give the very thing I need." Need more money? tithe or seek out ways to give financially; pay for someone's lunch anonymously, cover someone's movie ticket. Get creative.

I need favor. Cut the grass of the elderly couple next door. I need more friends. Find someone who can use a friend and be the very thing they need. If you do this in the right spirit not only will you feel amazing, but you'll totally enjoy watching (in awe) on how God begins to give back to you.

Secondly, check your heart. Motive is HUUUGE! with God. He will not be pimped. (I Samuel 16:7) Man looks on the outside, but God looks on the heart." If you want to stop failing, check your "why". If you're praying, serving, teaching or giving out of an attitude of self, then you might as well put your offering in a nice little pile and set it on fire.

(2 Corinthians 9:7) "God loves a cheerful, joyous, prompt to do it giver, who takes joy in their giving and God is able to supply all grace in abundance for every good work and charitable donation"

Before moving on to the next chapter, take a moment and check your motives. Why do I give? For years I gave out of pure guilt and fear. I gave because I thought God would "get me" if I didn't. No wonder I was a broke Christian, I wasn't cheerful nor was I joyous in my giving. As a result, there was absolutely no grace in my life.

Are you frustrated? Do you feel that you should be getting more out of God's promises? Then check your motives. You may be surprised by what you find. If you're still having trouble getting to the root of the issue, it may be time to talk to a professional. Message me on my Facebook Page and I can provide you with some help.

Slave Mentality VS. King Mentality

Awrong mindset is a huge reason as to why Christians fail. It's no wonder why the word of God constantly talks about being renewed in the spirit of our mind. (Ephesians 4:23) "We are new creatures behold old things are past away all things have become new. (2 Corinthians 5:17) "This means that anyone who belongs to Christ has become a new person. The old life is gone; a new life has begun." With so much talk about renewing our thinking, it makes you wonder? What's all the fuss about?

Pop Quiz! How can you get a king to think and act like a slave? Give up? Practice, Practice, Practice.

The enemy of our soul and spirit, is hard at work at one thing, to get you re-programmed to think and act like anything other than what you are, which is royalty and an heir of heaven and earth. The slave mentality is the perfect weapon because it's not only effective in sabotaging current tasks, but it is a living breathing spiritual organism that can replicate itself and infect entire generations long after you're dead.

While I would love to say that slavery is a thing of the past, it's not. Right now "human trafficking" is a global problem. From the sex trade here in the United States to forced labor camps in Dubai, China and portions of Africa, people and children are being bought and sold. We cringe at the thought of someone being dragged into such a life against their will but unfortunately many Christians are willfully entering into a form of spiritual and mental slavery without hesitation.

So, what does it mean to have a "Slave Mentality?"

Merriam-Webster defines Slave as "One that is completely subservient to a dominating force."

Take a moment and ask yourself, what's dominating my attention, finances, ministry etc? Congratulations you just found your slave master. Now what are you going to do about it? To get an understanding of how to get out of your own brand of slavery, it may help to know how you got in, to begin with. Here are some observations that may help.

1. A slave judges their environment by mirroring their master. If the master is happy, they are happy, if the master is upset, they are upset.

2. A slave strongly believes only in the value set by their master and despite their personal advantages and glaring qualities, the slave will not accept any other opinion about themselves other than those given by their slave master.

3. A slave believes that they live in a state of constant shortages and that the master is the only source of abundance. This is a powerful piece of manipulation because a sense of shortage keeps a person in a constant state of fear, worry and confusion which is ideal for slave masters because it helps stymie the threat of rebellion. Shortages also elevates the slave master to a god-like position.

4. A slave believes that there is no future. Many urban teens have been quoted as saying that they don't expect to live past the age of 23, while others say 18 years of age. If there is no hope for the future, then why invest in anything like community, savings, education or family. This explains why many poor and urban communities look more like war zones and shanty towns, while affluent neighborhoods are carefully planned with an eye toward the future.

5. Slaves don't ask questions or at the very least, not enough of them. There is a good reason for that. The word "why" Is the biggest threat to any master's authority, which explains why inquisitive thought leaders were often tortured, maimed or killed? These examples of violence caused many slaves to shun the desire to ask questions as well as undermine or attack another slave who made any attempt to ask questions themselves.

Why are questions so powerful? because they demand an answer. Why am I poor? Who said that this is all that I can do? Questions and dreams can get a person to see themselves operating in an environment in which a master is no longer relevant.

To anyone who deals in oppression and manipulation understands that taking away a person's desire to simply ask "why" is crucial. Why leads to dreams, dreams lead to hope, hope leads to plans, plans lead to action, and action leads to a dream fulfilled.

6. A slave believes that the master is the pinnacle of excellence and to be equal to them is to be superior. What's ironic is that this is farthest from the

truth. Lucifer was cast out of heaven, the ultimate "drop out." Adolf Hitler saw himself as the father of a master race but in the end, he was an incredible failure. This is the tragedy of setting the level of excellence by the standard of flawed individuals. Therefore, the pursuit to become equal to the oppressor is at best a "fool's errand." What if the women's movement changed their goal of equal pay for women to superior pay for women? By recognizing that the current standard set by the male workforce was substandard, women would have changed their standards and tactics based on achieving economic superiority not equality. So instead of competing for the corner office, they would focus on building a company that would buy the building with the corner office.

7. A slave mentality creates and cultivates an environment of constant uncertainty. Slave masters were always moving slaves around and disrupting their lives. At a moment's notice, day or night, men could barge in and take a child away, while the mother was assaulted with no threat of punishment. This state of constant wondering created an unintended

benefit for the slave master. In addition to fear, the slave mentality prohibited the slave from seeing the need to prepare, plant or plan for himself, his family or community. "Why build? they're just going to tear it down anyway."

8. To maintain this new normal of uncertainty, slaves within their own community would participate in the sabotage of another slave's attempt to create certainty. "Who do you think you are? Are you better than us?" The very oppression that we despised from the slave master was being done by the victims themselves; not because it was a good idea but because it was familiar. This is the reason why the rich get richer and the poor get poorer. The systemic barrage and abuse of this system takes you from hating it-to tolerating it-and eventually needing it.

9. A slave strives to hoard and maintain what they already have, this is carryover from a lifestyle of shortages.

10. A slave plays "Not to lose" They will not take risks and stick to the old methods even if they are outdated and no longer relevant.

11. A slave doesn't see themselves in authority or understands how it is used. As a result, that authority is abused and perverted until someone or something either takes it away from them or they offer it up willingly because he is unaware of its worth or its purpose.

So how do we move from a slave mentality to a King like mentality? See the below for some insight.

1. A king believes that they are a king, and this fact is both proclaimed publicly and drilled into the mindset of a child from birth. Daily, a prince or princess is intentionally reminded that he or she is a ruler from the time that they could understand, and every exercise is created to help look, think, and act the part. Being a King and having the mindset of one is an **intentional exercise.** The slave and king have this is common. One has a team of intentional abusers to tear him or her down, the other has a team of Intentional caretakers whose whole job is to build them up.

2. A king or queen seeks ways to constantly expand their kingdom and their influence

3. Kings play to win and expect to.

4. Slaves are fine with whatever, kings hold out for better or the best.

5. A king brings his kingdom everywhere he goes.

6. A king expects to affect the atmosphere and if it is substandard, they demand to be somewhere more suitable.

7. A king studies his authority, knows his authority and seeks to increase it.

8. Here is what the king and slave have in common. **They are both subject to the level of their mentorship and training.** Kings are assigned the best tutors, trained by the best marksmen and drilled by the best warriors. The slave is given the worst of everything, if given anything at all.

9. Much is expected from a king. Those expectation are huge and at times filled with pressure, but such pressure cultivates an emotional strength or EQ (emotional quotient) that allows him or her to handle themselves in high stress environments in which a decision needs to be made.

10. Kings, the good ones, are trained on how to be knowledgeable and cunning.

11. Kings do not expect fairness. They expect an unfair advantage.

The above is by no means an exhaustive understanding and description of what a slave or king is or isn't. There are exceptions to every rule. We have seen slaves who've become kings and visa-versa. We have seen good and noble kings and then we've seen very bad and treacherous ones. While training and mentorship are ideal, none of them are guarantees when it comes to getting the desired outcome. And while there is no perfect formula, the above provides us with some insight into the training used to generate two different destinies from one person.

Just think for a moment what your life would be like if you had a squad of people whose whole purpose was to pour into you all the tactics and skills needed to succeed. Now, imagine the opposite.

So how can a Christian use the above to create real change now?

Assuming for a moment that we all want to be kings as opposed to slaves, one has only to do the following. Believe – Decide – Commit - Repeat

Believe: You are a Christian (Christ-Like). He has written proof that you are his child and a joint heir with him with all rights and privileges. Your dad is a king and so are you.

Decide: Christianity Works! God works, and his word is true and If it's not working in my life, it's not His word, tactics or advice that's the problem, it's me.

Commit: Repeat this phrase: "I will commit to doing his Word until I have succeeded." Will it happen in 30 minutes or less, who can say? But it will happen sooner than you would expect if you don't quit. Your faith in Him and his will are the biggest factors in determining speed and nothing builds faith faster than reading His promises for yourself and getting around successful Christians who are winning in the areas that you seek progress in.

Notice that I didn't say to (get around a bunch of Christians). I said to get around successful Christians who genuinely have the victory in an area that you seek success in. This may be one person, it may be several. The point is you need to get around Christians who are winning. Please know that you are not limited to your local circle of believers, it could be an author or people that you follow on "YouTube" for example. Their habits, mindsets and rituals over time will rub off. Like the old saying goes "There's more caught than taught." So, seek to dwell among Christians with successful habits and eventually they will rub off on you.

Repeat: One of the biggest mistakes made by Kings is the refusal to continue in thy word. It's like a computer that refuses to receive the latest software patch or feature update. There is no such thing as "I've been a Christian for 20-years now and I have no more use for additional wisdom and instruction." Believe-Decide Commit-Repeat. The moment any part of that cycle stops, growth ceases and death will begin. When this happens even the strongest among us can lose sight of their authority and eventually lose their Kingdom.

Not Doing What You're Told

I f someone asked for a raise of hands on how many times you were told to do right but didn't, I would be on my back with both hands and feet in the air. Not doing what your told has turned into a cottage industry of sorts. Everywhere you go, your being told to question everything and everyone. Even politicians have gotten into the act by calling networks "fake news." Local citizens call leaders liars, leaders call citizens liars and the revolving door of distrust simply goes around and around. We are now living in a world in which no one wants to be told what to do, even if God himself says it.

For Christians this is a problem and yet another reason why they fail as often as they do. God is constantly speaking through pastors and teachers via social-media, television and of course at church. He's also speaking directly to us through our personal time of prayer, reading and studying.

But for all this talking and sharing, Christians and entire church communities are failing and losing their impact on themselves and the people they serve. Have we run out of good ideas? Nope. Does the word fail to deliver? Double nope.

We're failing to do what he's either told us to do or ignoring his word all together. It's a simple choice - Door Number #1. Do what He says, live an amazing life or choose Door Number #2: Don't do what he says and live a life full of fear discouragement and anger.

Deuteronomy 30:19: "I have set before you life and death, blessing and cursing, therefore choose life so that you and your children will live."

As a person who's spent a fair share of his Christian life failing, this is the one fact that I had to take ownership of. Behind every wrong turn and wrong decision was a person who (on purpose) ignored wise council, advice and repeated warnings to avoid trouble.

Your life is the sum total of every decision that you've made good or bad. Stop here and ponder this for a moment. Look at your health, your circle of friends and where you live. Your best ideas (and no one else's) got you here. How do you feel about that?

Now ask yourself, are you happy with those decisions? So many of us think in terms of big life events as the sole reason why our lives are where they are. Maybe it was a car accident, a job loss or winning the lottery. Those indeed are huge events that can have an immediate impact on our decision making. But if we only look at those milestone moments we'll miss the everyday thoughts that affect us the most.

I enjoy donuts. I think that many would agree that they are delicious and should be consumed early and often. However, a small decision to eat two donuts twice-a-week over the course of several years resulted in my inability to expose my sagging stomach at the local pool, find clothes that fit and feel confident about how I'm seen in public. Now I can tell you for a fact that I would have never thought that my weekly indulgence would have produced those results, but they did.

Our small decisions done over a period of time will create a "compound effect" in which small choices consistently made over time can and will produce a result. The question is, will you be happy with that result?

EXERCISE TIME:

1. Make a list of your daily routine.
2. What do you do when you get up?
3. What do you eat on a regular basis?
4. What you are listening to?
5. Who are you listening to? What do your friends look like?
6. Are you the only friend in this friendship?
7. What gets your attention on your social media timeline?
8. Do you have a set time with God and his word?

Write out your answers and say them out-loud. The impact of your answers are always strongest when you transfer them from out of your head and into the air. Now ask yourself, are you ok with the result? If not, what are you going to do about them? Do you want to do anything about them? Do you feel that you are powerless to change them?

For some of you, these answers are going to be shocking. If your reading this and the light-bulb has finally come on, then congratulations you're on your way to real change. But if you're saying great, what do I do now? or feel that you can use a little help, then message me and my team at Desmond Antonio Blackburn on Facebook or go to my website at www.layoffproof.com. We can help you by setting up a coaching session and getting you some one-on-one attention.

SIN MAKES YOU STUPID

ELDER AT LOCAL CHURCH EMBEZZELS $5,000 TO SUPPORT GIRLFRIEND

MINISTER SMOKES CRACK TO RELATE TO YOUTH GETS 3 YEARS FOR ROBBERY

CHURCH COUPLE DIVORCES OVER WIFE'S GIRLFRIEND AFTER BOTCHED THREESOME

I can go all day with examples of how blood-bought children of God have found themselves in the oddest of circumstances as a direct result of a sin area that was left unchecked and allowed to grow into a giant tumor of bad decisions.

How can this kind of thing happen to a believer? It's easy, they let it. Behind every bad decision made by a believer lies an area of sin in which that believer is convinced that there is no harm in indulging. Periodic visits to a porn site, telling white lies on an application etc. What they don't realize is that seemingly small actions like these corrupt reasoning and common sense. Wisdom and foolishness can't dwell in the same place and too many Christians believe that they can. After ignoring the conviction of the holy spirit their spiritual senses begin to harden against the word. As a result, bad is now good, good is now bad and the godly insight needed to see around the corner, is gone, leaving them to fight on your own with no covering. There's a name for Christians like that, they're called prey.

A Little Help Here.

O ne of the many reasons why we fail as Christians is because we either don't ask for help, feel that we don't need it or get the wrong kind of help all together.

When it comes to God's view on getting assistance, a few scriptures come to mind. (Genesis 2:18.) "Man should not be alone, for I will provide him a helper." (Matthew 8:20) "Whenever two or more are gathered in His name, there is he is in the midst."

Jesus recognized the need for help so much that one of his first moves was to go and assemble his team of 12 disciples to assist him in His work. In fact, before Jesus ascended into Heaven he told his disciples that he would not leave them helpless, but he would send the helper, aka the "holy spirit" (John 16:7)

Getting help isn't just a good idea, it's a God idea. Help is designed to empower us to simply get things done. A wise man once told me "Son you can get anything you want in this world, you just can't get it alone."

It's no wonder why the enemy of our soul, with a lot of help from our flesh, suggests that we isolate ourselves from people that can help us survive. It's simple, when you are isolated and alone you are vulnerable to attack and become nothing but prey to would be attackers.

There is safety in numbers. We have only to look at the animal kingdom to see this principle played out. The young deer is separated from the herd, it is then stalked and surrounded by mountain lions. The wounded calf that can't keep pace, is left behind and is attacked by wolves. The old eagle, who's beak is fragile and falls off can no longer hunt, starves and later dies alone.

These aren't just examples of life and death in the wild but a physical example of what happens to all of us when we buy into the lie, suggested by our demented life coach, that we're better off on our own. Clearly we are not.

In the word of God, the Devil is described as a ravenous predator, stalking and looking to and fro to see whom he may devour. (I Peter 5:8) This analogy is appropriate and speaks to the tactics of a true adversary. To get an understanding on how to avoid becoming prey to the enemy, it would be helpful to understand what prey looks like.

THEY ARE YOUNG:

When I was a "child I spoke and thought as a child. But when I became a man (mature) I put away childish things." (I Cor 13:11.) The young are most susceptible to attack when they have wandered off or fallen away from God's protective statutes, principles and common sense. Willful wandering is both irresponsible and reckless.

It's important to note that the "young" in this context isn't limited to age but understanding. There are many 40 and 60-year-olds who still haven't graduated from the 1st grade when it comes to maturity. As a result, the enemy is feasting on the young nubile flesh of the young and immature.

THEY ARE OFFENDED:

Taking on an offence whether personal, professional or spiritual is the fastest way to the "dinner plate" of your adversary. When a person is offended their first knee-jerk reaction is to lash out, to leave or to quit everything from their relationships to basic common sense. The lie being told sounds like this." I don't need them, I'm better on my own, etc."

People who've been offended are so distracted by the offence that they unconsciously create a blind-spot. When a person filters everything from the perspective of "how I've been wronged, disrespected or minimized" they become unable to see their part in the problem. The offended always sees themselves as the innocent party that did nothing wrong. When this happens the offended (unwittingly) puts themselves into a box and will not let themselves out until the person who offended them apologizes for their sin.

As you can see this new blind spot can make us one-dimensional, seeing only one possible outcome to a solution. The best way to guard against being offended is to ask yourself one question. Could it be me?

Now I'm not asking you to confess to every crime committed, neither am I asking you to roll over as soon as someone accuses you of something. Could it be me? simply allows you to take the focus off the circumstance and put it on you. Could it be me? Also opens the door to other questions that can help you see the need to change an approach in your mannerisms tone or physical posture.

I do a lot of speaking, over the years I've developed a very confident approach that is helpful in my efforts to command a situation or get people to recognize that I am leading a group or workshop. However, my authoritative style, speech volume and overall confidence, while helpful in some arenas sent another message in others. Some have felt that I can be intimidating and come on too strong, while others have felt that my mannerisms reminded them of a drill sergeant.

Because of these perceptions people began putting me in a box or assigning motives to me that weren't there. You could imagine my disappointment and at times, anger. For a while my first reaction was to lash out, but that got me nowhere fast. After listening to an instructor who challenged me to see myself from another person's point of view, I began to ask the question, could it be me? From that point on I started recording my speeches and coaching sessions. I even enlisted some colleagues of mine to give me some feedback on how I was seen and heard. Lastly, I began taking anonymous surveys. I was shocked at what I learned about myself. My emotions went from anger to understanding. I could now see what the people around me were saying and began to make changes.

By asking one question "could it be me?" stopped the offence from taking root and put the power back in my hand by allowing me to go to work, see my part in the problem and begin to make the necessary changes. If you're dealing with a similar situation in which you've felt misunderstood and your being seen in an unfavorable light I would encourage you to do what I did, OR you can continue to wait for those who've offended you to apologize. Good luck with that.

UNADAPTABLE

F ailure to adapt along with an unwillingness to adjust is another way that Christians fail. In the United States over 90% of all businesses will close in the first five-years. Emerging technologies are being created every six-months so, a slow to adapt mentality can send even a "man-bun", sandal wearing millennial to the back of the unemployment line. Now more than ever we need to adapt and fortify ourselves in both prayer and skill. The best way to do that is to look at the person in the mirror and get honest with your current situation.

Finding out that your "sweet" pony tail is no longer in style can be a little hard on the ego, but finding out that your prayer and praise time is old and useless is even worse. "Now I lay me down to sleep…" is an appropriate prayer for children but as an adult, not so much.

As our spiritual needs grow our spiritual fitness needs to keep pace. Noted evangelist and teacher Joyce Meyers teaches that Christians have to realize that with every new level there may be a new Devil" Now before we get bent out of shape, don't, this is how it's supposed be. It's called growth.

When you were in the 5th Grade, you learned all the state capitals but when you arrived in High School you began to learn Geometry. What happened? you grew and with every new grade level your capacity to take on new challenges and harder subjects grew as well.

As Christians, when it comes to recognizing our season of growth, we don't do so well. In the church sudden changes are often touted as an "attack" instead of an encouragement to step our game up. When we hear phrases like "new level-new devil," we forget that while there maybe a new challenge for our season. His "Grace" has also risen to meet the enemy where he is and dominate. In the words of Martha Stewart, "That's A Good Thing."

Doing Bad All By Yourself

Y ou can make an excuse for someone who may have
fallen on hard times due to an unforeseen tragedy
such as a natural disaster or act of violence. But what case
can you make for people who seemingly invite disaster by
choosing to ignore rules, statutes and outright warnings?

As I am writing this passage, Houston, Texas was
flooded by the damage caused by Hurricane Harvey. The
nation's fourth largest city was deluged by constant rain-
fall and found itself underwater in under 48-hours. Over
31 people died, and thousands were without power, dry
shelter or drinkable water, but that wasn't the tragedy.

The real disaster came before the storm when entire
families decided to ignore the warnings put out by state
and local authorities to evacuate and seek shelter else-
where. Many of those who stayed behind immediately
regretted their decision and although they were able to

escape with their lives, many were forced to reflect on their poor choices as they fled their flooded homes.

When we ignore the warning signs of the Holy Spirit and engage in "willful disobedience" the results can be devastating. We marry people that we shouldn't, and we start churches and companies that we have no business starting. Why do we do this?

> *"Proverbs (16:3) says to "Commit your actions to the Lord and your plans will succeed." In Job 5:12 it says "He frustrates the plans of schemers so the works of their hands will NOT succeed."*

When we get in the flesh as Christians and begin to devise and scheme without Him, we literally turn God from becoming our biggest ally to our greatest adversary. It's time that we get the revelation that *God Knows Everything And We Know Nothing.*

Once we understand our position, our walk with God will be amazingly simple and incredibly satisfying. Think about this for a second, the feeling of confusion and anxiety normally associated with making a correct decision will simply go away once you've put every thought or response through the filter of "What Does The Word Say?" Half the anxiety that Christians go through is due to our lack of patience because of bad choices and poor planning.

We need to simply "take a breath" and begin to practice our new position as Christians by consulting with the word of God and the Holy Spirit to walk in more confidence and less confusion. Secondly, we need to turn off our inner stopwatch when it comes to receiving from God.

When I was begging God to help me get married, it seemed that the more impatient I got, the longer everything took. My anxiety was at an all-time high. "When is he going to do it, is this the time?" When I finally got the revelation that only God could get me married then I switched my focus from begging and pleading to preparation.

I began reading books on marriage, how to pray as a husband and working on my career. I literally became so busy doing my job to prepare that I had no time to wonder if God was doing his. Shortly after making my commitment to start preparing for marriage, God opened the door for me to start dating the love of my life and within a year we were married.

When you talk to some Christians, you get the impression that they can get a faster response by going online instead of waiting on God. Why would a Christian feel this way? Because they have a closer relationship with Facebook Messenger than John 3:16.

According to an online article found in the *The Daily Mail* "Smartphone users check their Facebook account 14 times-a-day." The average Christian will boast that they read the word at least once a day for an average of 10-15 minutes. When you see statistics like this, the faith and confidence gap as it relates to God's word isn't that hard to understand. The stronger the relationship, the higher the faith, the weaker the relationship the weaker the faith, it's that simple.

EXERCISE

Close your eyes and imagine consulting with God at least 14-times per day regarding your family, finances or whatever. Now imagine what it would be like if you did this for five to seven days straight. Now open your eyes and answer some questions.

- Would your walk with God be deeper, about the same, or worse?
- Would your confidence in your ability to get a clear direction be higher, lower or about the same?

I think the answer is obvious that there would be a significant improvement to our confidence in God and his ability to get us results.

So allow me to encourage you to take this 14-times per day challenge. We'll make it simple. For the next 5 to 7-days, take a break for 60 seconds and simply pray or meditate on one of God's promises in an area where you have a pressing need and do this 14-times per day.

Now is there some kind of commandment that you will be breaking if you don't do this? Of course not. And neither should you feel condemned if you don't do this task 14-times a day. The point of this exercise is to force your flesh to stop resisting the need to "seek ye first the kingdom of God" and instead, jump into God's method of getting results with massive amounts of action.

Big Things Take Time

emanding that God move in 30-minutes or less to get you what you want is both immature, silly and unrealistic. Now I know that this is an exaggeration regarding time. But based on the stuff that we've said and done as Christians, you'd think that this was indeed the rule.

Another reason why Christians fail is our failure to understand that big things do take time.

"Lord why don't I have my mate yet? Why am I still in debt? When will this ministry take off? If you're a Christian, chances are you've questioned the speed in which God should have moved in a situation. Many have left the church in favor of another belief that promised a quicker path to success, only to find out that perception wasn't reality.

Can God move quickly? Of course, he can, and for anyone who's ever heard a testimony at church or on television, you can't help but become awestruck by the amazing power of God to move quickly and powerfully.

However, I'm suspecting that many of us in the church have seen and heard these testimonies and have walked away thinking that everything God does can be done in a blink of an eye.

Please keep in mind that there is nothing too hard for God and the outcome of a thing isn't nearly as valuable as the lessons learned along the way. I was recently reminded of this fact when I was thinking of my time spent in college. A university education takes about four-years to complete. This is common knowledge, so you could imagine the confused looks on people's faces when a freshman in college begins to complain that her degree is taking too long and that her plans for graduating at the end of the quarter will have to be delayed.

Back in the 90's when I was an aid to a city councilman in Los Angeles, California, I remember sitting in on monthly meetings called the Revitalization of Downtown Los Angeles. Back then, downtown Los Angeles wasn't very special. But in those meetings, people were planning, securing financing and networking 10-years before they broke ground on the Staples Center. Since then, downtown Los Angeles has turned into an urban mecca of shops, luxury hotels and housing and is known throughout the world as a desired place to do business.

So, we get it. When it comes to things of worth we know that big things can and do, take time. So why are Christians failing to stay the course and stay patient as they wait on God to do the big things in their lives? One of the main reasons is that we fail to create a tangible vision of what we want and what we are waiting for.

I love vision boards, here you can take photos and cut-outs of what you want and even post images of the people you admire and hope to become. I love this exercise because when people can see a thing, the mind treats it as real.

I remember listening to Arnold Schwarzenegger talk about putting the posters of famous body builders in his bedroom. Every day he would look at those posters and imagine himself winning the title of Mr. Olympia. He credited his practice of meditating on those posters as the main reason he was able to endure lifting, squatting and curling thousands of pounds. While others were angry about having to lift the weight, he said that he was excited because he knew that every rep would get him closer to greatness.

So, what's your vision?

Besides putting up a random vision-board filled with the images of "Nice to Have Stuff" create a vision board based on the character traits that your future self will need to dominate the next 10 – 20 years. Put a photo of yourself along with these character traits. To provide additional power, find a scripture that will correspond with each aspiration.

It's important to note that vision boards don't create action, action creates action. So, use your vision board to serve as a daily reminder on why you're taking the necessary steps to get obsessed

After disagreeing on almost every home that my wife and I saw together, I accidently came across a new housing development 30-miles from where we were living. Out of curiosity, I walked in. The models were amazing and immediately I could see our family living there. I brought my wife and kids the next day and everyone agreed that this was the house for us. The neighborhood was perfect, and the school rating was high. Although the pricing was out of our budget we began to go to work on our vision of getting into one of these homes. If this was God, he was going to make a way.

For two-years we went to work, paying down debt, improving our credit scores and educating ourselves on the home loan process. At least twice a week I would personally drive to this new area just to walk through the models. My vision was taking on a life of its own. I literally began to see myself getting off at "My Exit.", we were going to live here. I could feel it.

I was watching every show on HGTV with the intent on finding colors and designs that would work with our new home. I was obsessed. Then in 2011 the housing market was crashing in California. The same homes that were once out of reach, budget-wise, were coming down in price and we were in a prime position to take advantage of this opportunity. Our efforts over the last year to save, educate and improve our credit score seemed to have paid off. We purchased our home at a discount of $80,000 from its original list price. A strong vision coupled with Gods grace gets amazing results.

This is a lesson that I will never forget. Although it would take us two-years to be in the position to buy our home, our big vision forced us to put in the big effort needed to prepare for our tremendous gift. God has never been limited by time and yes, he can move in the blink of an eye. But like a good father he won't provide his kids gifts that they can't handle. The two-years wasn't an indicator of how fast

he can move but a measurement on how fast we can prepare to receive from Him.

Stop Casting Spells

I don't think that many people would consider themselves a witch especially if you're a Christian, so you could imagine my shock and amazement when I was accused of "casting spells." Now you may be wondering, who would say something like that? God himself.

In the late 90's I was living with other Christian men, helping the poor, teaching kids etc. How in the world could I be a witch, let alone cast spells? To be accurate, God's exact words were, "You are praying as if you are casting spells." Not one to leave you hanging, the Holy Spirit began to tell me what he meant by this, but before I do, allow me to back up. How did I get to this point?

Prior to this revelation I was a guy "In Love" (obsessed was more like it) with my current wife Denine. At the time of this writing we will have been married for 16-years. After about a year of dating we decided to cool things off so that we could get "closer to God." I know "super spiritual" right?

For me that idea lasted about two weeks before I wanted to get back together, but she was not having it. So, I turned to prayer. God was going to bring her back to me and prayer was going to be my weapon of choice.

I would pray for months. These one-sided prayer sessions were nothing more than a litany of complaints and whining sessions on why I felt God had to move on my behalf and give me what I wanted. I would pray for hours every night confessing scriptures regarding his promises.

At the time I was taught that if I continued to pray specific scripture over a desired area, that God would be compelled to give me the "desires of my heart."

I guess the Holy Spirit had enough. In a rare moment when I decided to stop petitioning and ordering God to obey his promises, I got quiet and waited to hear from Him. This is where he told me that my prayer sessions were like a witch casting spells.

This was very similar to the rebuke that God often made to the children of Israel. "Your worship me with your lips, but your heart are far from me." Another scripture in James 4:3 NLT: *"And even when you ask you DON'T GET IT because your motives are all wrong. You ONLY want what will give you pleasure."*

I was failing and for eight-years I was stuck and not getting any results because I was trying to pimp God into activating his promises. Motive is HUUUGE! with God. A right heart with the right motive are the activating agents needed to bring his promises to past. Those who deal in witchcraft seek to "hack into" or gain illegal access to the things of the spirit via drugs and deception to gain a result. This is error on a major level.

That rebuke was a huge wake-up call for me. After I apologized, I began to seek God by using the right motives regarding his will for my life. Don't get me wrong, I wanted to marry Denine in the worst way, but this time the obsession was gone and replaced with a freedom to simply trust him. After a season of working on my relationship with God, things got so good that I began to lose interest in the idea of getting married. Shortly after this revelation God would show me that he was opening a door to pursue Denine and in less than a year we were husband and wife.

So, what's the lesson? If you want to stop failing as a Christian and start living an accelerated life and see a move of God in your circumstances, then make sure your motives are in check. Ask yourself, is it about you or is it about doing what He said? Failure to recognize the difference will keep you circling the desert of frustration instead of enjoying the fruits of his favor in the promised land.

Move, You're In The Way

═══

In my opinion Christians all over the world are attending the longest running costume party ever known to man. Every day and especially on Sundays, we dress up and do our best imitation of what we believe a Christian should look and sound like. Unfortunately, we have extended our act to include prayer. When it comes to prayer we bring a "throw a lot to the wall and see what sticks" approach. Many people believe that If I pray enough times and string a bunch of scriptures together, God will supernaturally understand my intent and answer my prayer.

Matthew 6:7 "But when we pray, use not vain repetitions, as the heathen do: for they think that they shall be heard for their much speaking."

When I look back on my greatest breakthroughs seen in both my life and in the lives of others, they all have one thing in common, we got out of God's way. "Lord not my will, but thy will be done."

That's not just a phrase that reflects humility of heart but a positioning statement that declares that I am no longer going to allow my reasoning, doubt, fear, anger, unforgiveness, lust, jealousy, laziness, intellect etc. to get in the way of what you want done in my life.

It's so simple, it's profound. Jesus (God in the flesh) had his power (his ability to get results) hindered in places where people would simply refuse to get out of his and their own way. When he visited the home of his family, he said that he could not do many miracles, because of their unbelief. Jesus, while at the tomb of his friend Lazarus, tells his sister to not doubt but only believe" When she got out of her head and simply believed Jesus, her brother walked of his own tomb, alive.

Very rarely does someone associate their belief as the sole factor when it comes to receiving or not receiving from God. Instead we use excuses like: "It was my upbringing. I must have gotten lucky. The Universe has provided. This is an attack." etc. No matter the excuse, our unbelief continues to serve as the leading cause for failure in our Christian lives.

The power of belief is best illustrated in Jesus' exchange with the centurion whose young servant was ill at home and was about to die. When he stopped Jesus and explained his situation, Jesus asked where he lived and was willing to go with the centurion, but recognizing Jesus's authority the centurion told Jesus that as an officer when he gives a command to do something then it's done. He expressed that he expected no less from Him. Jesus was so impressed by the centurion's belief that Jesus declared from that moment that his servant would be healed.

The centurion's belief got him out of the way and gave Jesus a straight shot to delivering on His promises (not after a while or after several visits to rehab, but immediately) Now imagine this as a lifestyle, God says it and you, get out of the way. What do you think happens at this point? You automatically shift from the lane of "frustration discouragement and anger" and into the fast lane of results, encouragement and joy.

But Des how can you be so sure? I waited for my wife for nine-years. (not God's idea by the way) This was nine-years of me being stupid and immature by trying to hack into Gods promises. I finally stopped doubting and got out of God's way. When I did, we were married in under a year. God did more in 12-months than I did in nine-years!

I once needed money for bills due to a recent job loss. I prayed that morning and resolved to stop the worrying and walk in peace. I concluded my prayer at 7 a.m. and by 5 p.m. that afternoon I received a check in the mail. I looked at the postmark on the envelope and saw that it was dated several days before. God had already planned to deliver on his promise well before my morning prayer request. In this case He moved so fast it occurred the past.

Getting out of His way isn't just a super highway to seeing him move in our lives but a complete paradigm shift that blows the lid off man's belief that God's promises are slow and barely visible.

They are none of those things, we have only to believe.

Fail To Worship

I love worship. It's my favorite part of church service. To me worship is essential to preparing a person's heart and mind to not only hear a message from the pulpit but to hear the part that is specifically intended for me. I can't count the number of times that I've felt that a sermon was specifically written just for me. It's as if someone was reading my mind and took note of every gripe and then answered it.

Praise is an amazing expression of my heart when it's difficult to pray. Let's face it, sometimes you just don't know what to say. You look up, open your mouth and all you can hear is uh, uh, uh! When this happens all it takes is a simple word like "Thank You" or "You're Good" and before you know it, your face down on the carpet in full blown worship.

Maybe that's the reason I love it so much. I can honestly say that there has never been a time in which I was not able to enter into worship and not feel better. Worship is many things and one of them is "transformational."

The ability to take a state of mind and totally change it from sadness to joy without the use of anti-depressants or medical marijuana is invaluable in this day and age. Worship is powerful but incredibly misunderstood by believers, which is another reason why Christians fail; we fail to worship.

If you grew up in the church during the 70's and 80's you may have seen a few things. To begin with, worship was viewed as a form of Christian entertainment. Whether you were Baptist, C.O.G.I.C, Pentecostal or whatever, worship was done "to you" by the choir.

Our job as the congregation was to simply react like those who attended a concert. Every now and then we'd yell "Yes Lord!" and do a gospel version of the river dance whenever the organist got hot. It's no wonder why so many of us grew up clueless on how to worship God in church, let alone in private.

Worship was also seen as emotional, something that would only appeal to folks in touch with their feminine side. Unless you were the pastor, the mens' facial expressions showed very little tolerance. Do they hate the song? Are they angry, who knew? This example screwed me up as a young man, "Should I stand up and clap or sit and scowl?" I was confused all the time.

On the other extreme you saw your Methodists, Catholics, Episcopalians and Lutherans take a more stoic approach. Their worship was quiet with opera like hymns that were sung by the psalmist. In these services the congregation is encouraged to react to a ritualistic call and response from the psalmist or priest. There is no entering into his presence. In this environment worship had to demonstrate extreme reverence. This isn't a bad thing, but in these environments, worship was so heavy on process and light on joy, that WHO they were worshiping wasn't nearly as important as HOW they were worshiping.

With so much confusion around worship it's a miracle that any of us went to church at all. In the last 20-years, we've seen an amazing movement in which choirs have had their roles enhanced from that of Christian entertainment to that of "worship leaders" who lead the congregation into God's gates with thanksgiving and into his courts with praise.

Although we haven't totally arrived, we're a lot farther along than we were. Now it's time to take advantage of this mighty weapon of warfare. Praise does many things to help us win. Think of it as the three C's: Clarity, Courage and Confidence.

Clarity: Praise is phenomenally effective in helping take the focus off of our failures and back on God who can solve our problems. It's a medical fact that stress releases a hormone called Cortisol into your body and mind. When you and I get worried it's almost impossible to think creatively or think at all. Praise can transform the body on a cellular level by retarding the release of Cortisol into our system and releasing hormones like Serotonin, Endorphins and Dopamine that promote both calm and feelings of happiness.

Courage: Prov 28:1: "The wicked run away when no one is chasing them but the godly are as bold as Lions." It is said that Joshua, when leading an attack against the walled city of Jericho was instructed to put the musicians ahead of the army. In warfare, that move was revolutionary after all, soldiers fight and musicians play instruments. You know the story, they marched around the city seven times and then with a loud shout of voices and instruments the walls came tumbling down.

As Christians we neglect this weapon. Our time of praise and worship can get us to a place where we see what God sees regarding our circumstance. Praise changes your very state of mind. What seemed hopeless, at first. is now met with boundless optimism and enthusiasm.

Confidence: Prov 3:26: "For the Lord is my confidence and he will keep my feet from being caught."

Praise and worship creates intimacy between you and God. Secrets are shared, inside jokes are created. You feel that you know Him and that He knows you. You've spent so much time together in worship that you not only feel confident, but you feel safe.

Many would agree that confidence in a person or institution is either built up or torn down largely based on the level of their relationship. The deeper the relationship the stronger the trust, the weaker the relationship the weaker the trust.

Despite our baggage with the church, the real reason while we are failing in our effort to receive all that God has for us is that we don't know Him. And where there is no knowledge, there is no confidence. Well I've got great news, praise and worship can change all of that. One of the ways to build confidence after being burned before, is knowing that no matter what I do, I can't get hurt again because it's impossible to get hurt in his presence.

If getting clarity, walking in courage and living with more confidence are your goals, then commit right now to the "7 FOR 7 Challenge." For seven days for seven minutes simply commit to giving God your un-divided attention and give him praise. Whether you know a praise song or not, isn't material. Use this time to get into a freestyle attitude of gratitude. For seven minutes thank Him for life, parents, ideas, non-fat lattes, whatever. Do this for seven days for seven minutes. When the seven days are over go to my facebook page Desmond Antonio Blackburn and tell me about your experience. My guess is, your experience will be nothing short of extraordinary.

UNTEACHABLE

I f I had to characterize my 20's with just one word, "UNTEACHABLE" would be at the very top of the list.

As a parent I've been part of a lot of conversations in which the phrase "If someone had only told us." has come up from time-to-time. But I must confess, it wouldn't have mattered if I was taught the very lessons of life on a "Jumbotron" at Dodger Stadium. My pride and overall arrogance made me so unteachable that I was fully convinced that I already knew everything at age 17.

Every Sunday millions of Christians gather around the world to sit down and learn about the teachings of God by an assortment of ministers and scholars. While they sit and pretend to listen, many are distracted as they update Facebook or check in with Twitter. But what's really going on is a coordinated and self-inflicted form or blindness that says that the word of God does not work with my 21st century lifestyle. Right now, my social media timeline, filled with dancing cats and fake friends are way more relevant than learning about Christ.

So what does it mean to be unteachable? What does it look like? Kenneth Kuykendall, author of the blog "Pastoral Ponderings" outlines the 7-traits of an unteachable person this way:

1. No spirit of humility
2. No hunger for wisdom
3. Closed eyes and clogged Ears
4. A Closed mouth (doesn't ask questions)
5. A negative outlook
6. No desire to be around growing people
7. No willingness to apply what they have learned

I love this check list because men and women of God who've looked into the mirror and said "Could it be me? Could I be the problem?" have been able to identify their shortcomings and take ownership of their lives. When this happens an easier path to real change takes place and victory is all but guaranteed.

When a person is un-teachable they enter the "Un-realm." For those unfamiliar with what "Un" means it is a pre-fix that means "Not". When a person is Un-teachable they are NOT-teachable NOT– reachable NOT-favorable, NOT-remarkable, NOT-reliable, NOT-dependable and most of all NOT-aware that they are unteachable. People who suffer from this affliction cannot see that they are standing in their own way.

So, what can be done about it? How can a person who isn't teachable, become teachable? I've got two words for you, Pain and Prayer (in that order)

Pain:

Speaking from personal experience, pain can come from a huge event or a series of very humbling ones. These events can get a person to take a long hard look at themselves. These experiences are often traumatic and can force a person to see that what they've believed about themselves was nothing more than a stack of well positioned lies wrapped in bow of silly-string. This is one of those moments in which you come face-to-face with the revelation that you are full-of-crap and this time it's not ok.

Prayer

Turning to prayer when you've finally reached the point of humility and brokenness will be the most freeing and honest time that you will have with the Lord. In fact, if you listen closely you can almost hear Him say "can you hear me now?"

Psalm 51:17 "The only sacrifice that I desire is a broken spirit and contrite heart."

"But I don't understand, I've prayed plenty of times before, didn't God hear me, then?" It's more like you wouldn't hear him. Unteachable people in prayer are prone to monologues in which there are plenty of petitioning and not much else. True prayer is a conversation in which you are looking to hear from God after you've petitioned Him. God in his love is extremely patient and will wait to be invited to speak.

I can remember spending hours in a garage praying to God about everything I wanted and thought I needed. This went on for years. However, this time things were different. After a disastrous number of setbacks, I came before him broken and receptive. All I wanted was to simply hear from Him and sure enough he began speaking to me. Once I removed myself and let God do most of the talking. I got clarity, confidence and courage.

Jumped To Soon /Stayed To Long.

During my brief stint in politics, I worked for a local Assemblyman in Southern California. It was a good job that had me thinking that perhaps politics was going to be a new career choice for me. However, six months into the job I began to get an urging in my spirit to leave. But I thought to myself why should I leave? I was doing well, I was well liked, and the pay was decent. In less than a year I was fired. What happened? I ignored the witness of the holy spirit and stayed too long. It would take another 17-months before I found another position.

In another example, I wanted to be in a relationship and I wanted it now. I was tired of waiting on God and decided to take matters into my own hands. I met a girl, turned on my charm and got her to go on a date with me. During this time, I can feel God telling me to break it off since it was out of his timing. Angry and arrogant, I ignored the witness. Needless to say, the date went poorly and I never saw her again. To make matters worse, my rebellion hurt my relationship with God and it delayed my chances to get with Denine for another year. So much for taking matters into my own hands. I jumped too soon.

Timing is everything when it comes to God. As Christians, we believe that just because I'm a believer, decisions can be made to move in our own time and God will find a way to work it out. This form of thinking is ineffective and less than ideal.

Case in point: Abraham is given a vision that he would have a son with Sarah who couldn't have children. Sarah, out of frustration, moves out of God's timing by giving Abraham her handmade to have a son through her. Although Sarah would eventually bear Abraham a son on her own, the child that he fathered out of God's timing grew up to become an enemy of the promised child and now we have a war between Jews and Islam that has lasted for centuries. When man tries to help God "move things along", the result is always destruction, damage and delay.

When I think about this mentality of staying too long or jumping too soon I think about toddlers. Anyone who's ever watched a child learn to walk or crawl for the first time knows that this can be a full-time job keeping them away from potential danger. In a moment they'll leap, jerk or run out of a room with no regard for boundaries or potential danger.

As Christians we leap, jerk and run out of the grace of God's timing with no regard for boundaries hoping that when we run into danger, God will protect us. As you can imagine, this type of presumptive thinking has cost many Christians their calling and in some cases, their lives.

Jesus recognized this tactic when Satan tempted Him after he had fasted for 40-days. Satan asked him to prove his God-like power by throwing himself from off the mountain, "Surely the Angels would catch you before your foot dashed against the stone." Jesus refused. Why? Because he feared heights? of course not. Jesus was showing Satan a couple of things. First, he didn't need to prove anything and second, the devil isn't the boss and unless the boss says to move, you don't move. This wasn't just an example of obedience but common sense. I only win when I obey God. When I move without Him and his grace I lose time and most of all, I lose the advantage.

Check out the scenarios below, do they sound familiar?

- You start a business and consult with everyone but God and go bankrupt in under a year.

- You consult with God, get insight on a little-known start up idea and now you're a millionaire in under a year.
- You date a person and eventually get married. You ignored all godly counsel to avoid marrying this person and now the marriage is struggling to survive.
- You express your desire to change jobs. You ask God for his timing and you end up getting an amazing offer in an industry that you love.
- You ignore a witness to leave a job and stay because of the health benefits, now the job is gone and so is your health plan.

So, what's the lesson here? You make better moves with God than without Him.

If He's Not First Your Last

It's poor manners to begin a meal until the guest of honor arrives first. If that person happens to be royalty, such a violation could land you in jail or worse. In our lives we understand the importance of setting the right tone or putting things in its proper order to get a result. You wouldn't start a toddler on a diet of steak and potatoes before they had teeth, would you?

One of the reasons why Christians fail is because we've become so cavalier in our approach to God and his promises that when we "technically" speak His word, it falls flat and fails to deliver any real results. What happened? Was God unable to deliver on his promise? Of course not, but your request, may have failed to activate because of a poor understanding of God's divine order. (1 Cor 14:40) "Let all things be done decently and in order."

Going to court and standing before a judge is a prime example of our need to do things God's way. Anyone who's ever gone to court can tell you that it's all about the rules of conduct and procedure. In most court rooms, you can't even speak to the judge unless you follow a specific protocol. There is a dress code to be in their presence and for others, there is a procedure before speaking to the judge "May I approach the bench?" And in all cases, the judge is never referred to by their name but always by "Your Honor."

But following the protocols aren't enough when making a case before a judge. The attorney must be persuasive and passionate. His case must also be solid and complete with facts that can be backed up with case law. Mindless rambling is penalized, and conclusions based on assumptions are often thrown out.

Standing before a judge is serious and understanding how to do so could be the difference between going to jail or going free. But when it comes to the creator of heaven and Earth our approach is so casual that its really no surprise why many of our prayers are "Dead on Arrival."

Now I know what some of you may be thinking. Now Des we've been redeemed from the curse of the law and we are now under grace. After all, a lot of the ceremonies and sacrifices that were required back in the day are no longer required to speak to God. And while this is true, it was also incomplete. Let me explain.

At the core of every ceremony was a purpose filled attempt to demonstrate our honor for God and all that He has done. These ceremonies put God first and celebrated His greatness. These ceremonies provided man with an opportunity to declare to the world "Hey I prefer God and he's worthy of my best." His desire to be honored hasn't gone away. God still wants that from us. (Matthew 6:33) "But seek ye first the kingdom of God and all these things shall be added unto you."

For years I judged my ability to get results from God based on my knowledge of his word and my ability to artfully use them when needed; but as I've gotten older in the things of God I can see that my understanding has been incomplete.

God wants us to give him the preferential treatment that he so richly deserves. For years man has missed the true intent of these ceremonies. The ceremonies never gave God any value. they were simply vehicles that put us in position to prefer God and when we did, it activated God's ability to provide the extraordinary results that we've been looking for.

STOP RIGHT HERE!

Do you know what you just read? This is it! This is the key to no longer failing. Giving God preferential treatment is intentional, especially when it's coming from a sincere place of honor and not mindless obligation promoted through religion. Let's stop limiting God to a pre-trip prayer or grace at the table. Let's bring him into the boardroom meeting, before a test or on a date. Without God, plans don't succeed. So what are we waiting for? It's time to stop bringing a butter knife to a gun fight and pull out the BIG GUNS of his grace and favor by simply giving him the head seat when it comes to making every-day decisions.

Getting You To Stop, The Real End-Game

What is the end game? I believe that (Galatians 5: 7-8) gives us some insight in this area "You did run well, who did hinder you that you should not obey the truth? This persuasion does not come from the one that called you."

Think about this for a moment, isn't "stopping" the most common outcome experienced by believers whenever sin is present?

- When you get depressed, you stop going to church, you stop working out, you stop meeting with friends and family etc.
- When you get offended: you refuse to get it straight with the other party and stop trying to make it right.
- When you get intimidated by the moment, you stop trying to breathe, you stop performing. You stop pushing forward.

Take a moment if you can and "skip to the end" of your current issue or dilemma. I don't want to project anything unto you but ask yourself this question, what did I "stop" as a result of that situation or conflict? What did I put on hold "until I've figured things out?"

It is a widely held notion that humans express one of three responses in times of fear, they call it flight, fight or freeze. While the first two are the reactions that are most talked about, freezing up is what many of us experience on a regular basis. All you have to do is pull up the subject "stage fright" on YouTube and you will see what I am talking about.

I must admit that some of these videos featuring people who've frozen up on stage can be entertaining. But freezing or suddenly stopping, if only for a moment can be incredibly dangerous. The enemy of our soul knows that if he can coach you to freeze every time you're presented with an opportunity to step out of your comfort zone, then he's got you. Freezing gives Him just enough time to get you to sabotage yourself.

John Maxwell, noted Christian author and speaker in the area of leadership once said "Growth is our only guarantee that tomorrow will get better." Growth is intentional and being intentional requires movement. Anyone will tell you that a stationary target is easier to hit, while a moving target isn't.

It's my belief that Christians are failing in a massive way because we've allowed the enemy to coach us into stopping long enough to allow him to have a clear shot at not just our hearts and minds but our momentum.

So what do we do about it?

In Mel Robbins book "The 5 second rule" she shares a technique that she used to trick her brain into acting and getting beyond the self-sabotaging effect of hesitation, she did a count-down. While dealing with a bankrupt business, career failure and a marriage that was in trouble, simply getting out of bed for Mel was becoming a challenge. One

HOW TO FIRE THE DEVIL AS YOUR LIFE COACH!

day, while watching a space shuttle launch, she heard mission control start their count down 5, 4, 3, 2, 1. Desperate to use anything to help deal with her depression and simply get up, she began to do her own countdown every morning by saying 5,4,3,2,1. Get up!

This became her daily ritual. Noticing how this little tactic was helpful in getting her out of bed, she began to expand this new technique into every area in which she would normally hesitate. Before long, her new tactic started to breathe new life into her day-to-day. She began doing more, her marriage improved, she was working out, writing books, consulting etc. all because she used a simple tactic to interrupt a habit of hesitating and replaced it with one that told her brain and emotions to simply move forward.

As Christians, we have the tools needed to not only interrupt but reprogram how we respond when tempted to hesitate. Ever hear of the Holy Spirit? Yeah, he can do this. Keep in mind that his main job is to conform us into the image of Christ, so the power is there to make a change. The question is, are we willing to use that power?

One of the ways to use this power is to get educated about our authority and the weapons afforded to us. It's kind of hard to fire a gun when you're holding it like a banana. It's even harder to win your fight against hesitation when you are purposely feeding on the media and hanging out with those who are constantly reminding you of all the ways that you can fail. "I wouldn't do that if I were you. Are you sure this will work? Are you even qualified? what if you fail, then what?" It's time to ditch the zeroes and find some heros.

After moving into our new home, I found myself in a new community with new neighbors and no friends. Needing fellowship, I actively started praying to the Lord to help me "Find My Tribe." I needed to have energetic, men and women of God who were fun, adventurous and entrepreneurial and who were my age. I also began to change my habits by bombarding my mind with specific scripture around the areas where I was having the biggest challenges.

I said bombard, not casually study. If your serious about getting out of this death spiral of hesitation, then you need to unlearn how to hesitate and learn how to walk in boldness. Now you don't need to know 8,000 scriptures about your area, but you do want to learn and openly confess those four or five scriptures over yourself. It should be confessed so often that it is literally the first thing you think of when you are challenged.

Secondly, you need to fight more. We can shadow box all day with great skill but here's the problem, shadows don't hit back. For Christians like you and I we need to relish our opportunities to fight. As I've gotten older and had a chance to reflect, I've realized that the times in which my confidence was highest was right after a period of intense conflict. It was also in these times in which I was able to put my fears, prejudices and ridiculous opinions to the test. I admit, I've gotten my "head bumped" many times. I came face-to-face with my foolish thinking, judgmental attitudes and wrong motives. I was humbled repeatedly, and I am better for it.

I don't want to paint a picture of puppy dogs and rainbows for you, but teachings that create an expectation that a successful walk with God is devoid of pain and adjustments are just wrong. I'm sure that some Christians may mean well, but the fact is, that's just not God's way.

(James 1:2-4 NLT) "Dear brothers and sisters when troubles of any kind come your way, consider it an opportunity for great joy. For you know that when your faith is tested, your endurance

has a chance to grow, so let it grow, for when
your endurance is fully developed you will be
PERFECT, COMPLETE, NEEDING NOTHING."

We're failing as Christians because we've bought into this lie that if we're living a good life devoid of any serious conflict, then we're doing it right. I'm not sure what Bible you're reading but from the time that Jesus was born everyone from his parents to his disciples experienced constant drama. Whether it was escaping the assassination attempts from King Herod to avoiding the jealousy of religious leaders, crisis was always present, but so was God's Grace.

As a kid living in Brooklyn, New York I had an unreasonable fear of being hit in the face and knocked out. To me this risk was simply too high and based on the empirical evidence shown on boxing bouts that I witnessed on television, getting knocked out was a very real possibility.

Scared of my own shadow, I would avoid conflict at all costs, and when threatened I would immediately cower. One day while attending the first week of high school, I simply said hi while passing another student and without warning he threw a punch that landed on my face. I was shocked! but not by his punch. I was shocked because I was hit in the face and did not immediately die. I distinctly remember thinking to myself, "huh, that wasn't so bad." Thankfully someone came by and broke up the fight.

Now most people would be upset, after all this jerk just tried to make me go "night-night" in front of my friends. But not me. I was oddly happy and relieved. I just took a punch and did not die.

That fight was the best thing to happen to me. I found my confidence and all my silly fears where seen for what they were, nothing. I believe that this is what the word means in (Psalm 23:4) "***Yea though I walk through the valley of the shadow of death, I will fear no evil.***"

We need to have these walks, we need to have these fights, because without them we'll continue to act like scared little children cowering at the mere threat of conflict and succumbing to the enemy's true end game which is to get you and I to stop moving long enough to be nothing more than target practice.

So What Have We Learned Boys And Girls?

I t takes courage to realize that you're not the victim you thought you were. Finding out that you've intentionally or un-intentionally hired the Devil as your life-coach can be a bit surprising, especially as a Christian. Now before we get caught up in any guilt or condemnation DON'T! It's a complete waste of your time and you get no points for it.

But you do get points for acting. The first action step is to simply hit "stop" and start over. And the best way is by saying this prayer out load.

"Devil, your fired! God your hired! "I've realized that I've been intentional in my efforts to avoid doing things your way. But I see now that I was wrong the entire time. Lord you are my God and I want to do things your way. I want to be the best version of myself and only you can make that happen. I reject everything that is not you and

I acknowledge you as my Lord and Savior Jesus Christ. Come into my heart, make me new. In Jesus name, amen."

If you've said that prayer, can you let me know? Go to my Facebook page and message me. I want to both encourage and help you to get you connected to a great church in your area.

Furthermore, it's important to note that while you've fired one coach, it's time to hire another one. You need to invite Jesus back into your affairs. A simple, "God, what do you think?" would be a great start. Secondly, find a great church that is teaching the word in a way that is both easy to understand and easy to apply to your life.

But Des! I'm a Christian who can use a little help. I need accountability, I need a plan and I need some technical hand holding that will help me to stop getting in the way of my business, ministry and marriage is there anything besides this book that can help me?

Recently, everyone from pastors to Christian business people have been employing the services of Christian Life Coaches. This community of professionals are trained and certified to help leaders stay on track with their vision while helping them get out of their own way. This is not counseling, but a powerful tool to help leaders stay accountable.

DESMOND ANTONIO BLACKBURN

As a certified Christian life coach, my team and I have helped men and women to get back on track when it comes to walking in the fulness of their purpose.

So ask yourself?

- Do you have a lot of unfinished projects?
- Do you tend to start with a bang and end with a fizzle?
- Do you do your best work when you are held accountable
- Are you done with "Do It Yourself, Self-Improvement."

As a parent, author and speaker, life gets busy and having someone to hold you accountable to your vision has become mission critical in this world of increasing distractions and creative excuses. After two-years of saying that I wanted to write this book, I gave up on "will power" and decided to hire a coach to help me finish this book. Well here we are. I guess it worked.

If this sounds like you or someone you know contact me, via Facebook at Desmond Antonio Blackburn or go to www.howtofirethedevilasyourlifecoach.com and I'll schedule a session with you. The first session is at no charge. From here, I can begin to help you see where the blocks are and how to remove them.

Am I Ready To Get A Coach?

Christian Coaching is not for the casual observer who is looking to "try something new." Coaching is for people who've decided to waive the white flag and give up on trying to solve a problem on their own.

For example: An event planner who's amazing at organizing events but refuses to charge enough money to pay the bills or themselves. Or the mix martial arts gym owner who can fight any man at any time, any-where, but can't find the sales confidence to tell others about his gym.

In both cases, these people have tried to change on their own but are experiencing mental or emotional blocks that are keeping them from charging what their worth and telling others about their services.

Coaching is also for people who have a clear understanding of how much they are losing as a result of their barriers.

In the case of the event planner, she estimated that she was losing at least $50,000 per year in revenue due her hesitation to charge what she was worth. In the case of the gym owner, he knew that if he could increase his sales confidence, the gym could bring in an extra $5,000 per month.

As a sales professional for the last 30 years I've specialized in coaching entrepreneurs, authors, teachers and pastors who've all realized that their inability to first sell themselves on their own vision, was the number one reason why they are not making the progress that they needed. These people have come face-to-face with the realization that its not the competition, the economy or their products, but it was their inability to shake off some "bad code" that kept them from selling.

If this sounds like you or someone you know then go to www.layoffproof.com or message me at Desmond Antonio Blackburn on Facebook and we'll get you scheduled for a free 30-minute coaching session.

The Finish Line

Allow me to be the first to congratulate you. ***"Firing the Devil As Your Life Coach"*** is just the beginning and while hiring a Christian life coach is helpful, the most important thing that you can do is reconnect with your relationship with God.

In case you don't know what that looks like allow me to illustrate. It's a relationship in which you are doing more listening and learning than you are begging for favors.

Secondly, begin to get into worship. Unlike any genre of music, worship's ability to transform you from one state to another is nothing short of amazing.

Worship is one of the best and fastest ways to really know God at His Core. No need to align your Chi, light any candles or purchase any orange jumpsuits. Worship helps a person (really) change. So many of us have said, well until I've gotten clean or start living right then I'll get back to church. You've got it backwards.

When I first started working out with an MMA trainer he would demonstrate the moves that I would one-day hope to make on my own. I witnessed the strength of his punches and kicks. It didn't take me long to understand that his slender frame and lack of a gut was one of the reasons why those kicks and punches were being done with such power. This was my incentive to change my diet. If I had any chance of getting strong and becoming fit, then my addiction to bad eating had to go.

It works the same way in worship. Come as you are. If you cuss a little or a lot, have marital issues or any other problems then get into worship. The longer you do it the more you'll begin to change (On your own) Before long you'll be throwing off your desires to smoke weed, watch porn, cheat etc., not because your feeling guilty due to the sermon given by the preacher, but by an insatiable desire to get closer to God because of worship. If worship is new to you, go to youtube and type in the artist "Israel and New Breed, Phil Tarver, Micheal W. Smith and Hillsong Worship.

WARNING!

Worship isn't magic, but a strategy. This won't instantly cure your desire to watch porn but trust me, watching porn will become less appealing after entering his presence.

Why? will the images change? no, but your taste and desires will the longer you spend time with God. Worship, coupled with a good church and some form of online or in church "Life Group" will be just what the doctor ordered. Reach out to me on Facebook and I can help get you pointed in the right direction.

Lastly, find your tribe. If you're a stay at home mom, busy entrepreneur, a new dad or an empty nester trying to find new meaning since the kids moved out, reach out to your ministry and inquire about your need to get around some like-minded folks. Trust me, with a planet of almost seven-billion people, your tribe of those who share your world view and experiences are out there.

If your ministry doesn't have a life group, then find one that has. If moving isn't an option at this time, then let your fingers do the walking. Access YouTube channels for your group and become a part of a Facebook team of believers who share your experience and lifestyle. Thankfully in today's social media environment, help is a mouse-click away.

Thank You

I t's been my honor to serve you and I hope that this book has helped. If you've liked what you've read I would love to hear from you. I can be found on Facebook at https://www.facebook.com/desmond.a.blackburn/. Here you will have access to both my "Two-Minute-ish Drills." Along with my new show, "DOERS" which can be viewed every Friday at 8 a.m. P.S.T.

I speak quite often and would love to come to your group, business or ministry. If you've been blessed and feel that this would be the ideal subject for your organization then reach out to me. We can set up a call and get a better idea of what you and your group are looking for.

Lastly, I am a certified Christian Life Coach. I specialize in helping entrepreneurs, authors and ministry leaders identify the blocks that are keeping them from breaking out of the old stories and bad code that they've picked along the way.

Your purchase of this book comes with a free 30-minute Christian Life Coaching session. I would encourage you to take advantage of this. Coaching is becoming the "go to" solution for everyone from athletes to sales executives, authors and anyone looking to both get and keep the "edge." Schedule a session today so that you can experience what one-on-one coaching can do for you.

About the Author:

Desmond Antonio Blackburn is a professional speaker and author of three books, *"Layoff Proof, They Will Buy From You and How To Fire The Devil As Your Life Coach."* He is also the founder of "The Blackburn Affect" a faith based new business and sales coaching firm. He is also the daily host of the "2-minute-Ish drill and #DOERS, a Facebook live program that airs every Friday at 8 a.m. PST.

Desmond is a lifelong entrepreneur, frustrated comedian and self-professed movie nerd. He is the father of two amazing children Kyle and Chloe and husband to his wife Denine. He's a Christian who is obsessed with showing the world that everyday men and women who know God, can and must the abundant life outlined in His word.

For questions about speaking appearance or to schedule a one on one session with a Christian life coach please go to www.layoffproof.com or message Desmond Antonio Blackburn on Facebook.